Inclusion

in the primary classroom:

support materials for children with autistic spectrum disorders

SL

We are often asked:

'Why should I do all this for ONE child in my class?'

We believe that the ideas and strategies we suggest will benefit all the children in the class.

The National
Autistic Society

Published by The National Autistic Society

Designed by Cottier & Sidaway

Reprinted in 2009

Printed by Newnorth Print Ltd

ISBN 978 1899 280 95 7

Welcome!

Primary Inclusion
for children with autistic spectrum disorders

Aims

- To provide practical support for mainstream staff working with pupils who have autistic spectrum disorders (ASD) including Asperger syndrome

- To draw together a range of research theories, strategies and approaches

- To give staff a basic understanding of autistic spectrum disorders

- To disseminate tried and tested methods which can be of benefit to all children

Contents

Autism and Asperger syndrome   2

Adapting the curriculum and the learning environment   6

Using visuals   10

Promoting positive behaviour   18

Sources of information   38

Autism and Asperger syndrome

What is autism?

The Concise Oxford Dictionary defines autism as a 'condition usually present from childhood, characterised by complete self absorption and a reduced ability to respond to or communicate with the outside world'.

The condition was described by Leo Kanner in 1943. He believed that autism resulted from problems occurring in the developing brain – initially many parents do not notice that their child is not developing in the same way as other children but around the age of 2 to 3, when generally there is a great improvement in social skills and communication, the child's developmental differences become more obvious.

Some children in mainstream schools may have a diagnosis of Asperger syndrome. Hans Asperger first described this condition in 1944 but his work was not published in England until 1991. Asperger syndrome is commonly referred to as being on the 'autistic' or 'autism spectrum'.

To have a diagnosis of autism the child must have:

● difficulty with social relationships

● difficulty with social communication

● impaired imagination and creative play.

These are referred to as 'the triad of impairments'. The child must have difficulties in all three areas for a diagnosis of autism to be made.

All children are different and the way autism affects the individual is very variable so the term **autistic spectrum disorder** is often used to describe the condition.

A diagnosis of autism does not reflect anything about intelligence but describes how much the child exhibits the autistic behaviour. A highly intelligent child, for example, could display extreme autistic behaviour whereas a child with a lower intelligence may display only mild autistic behaviours and vice versa.

Lorna Wing, an expert on autism, describes the disorder along a continuum

Social relationships

Mild difficulty	Can initiate interaction Has difficulty coping in group situations Has difficulty 'reading other people's minds' Lacks empathy
Moderate difficulty	Tolerates interaction but does not seek social situations
Severe difficulty	Not interested in social contact Unaware people have different thoughts to their own

Communication

Mild difficulty	Talks about subjects based around their own interests Does not take account of the listener and often continues to talk when others are not interested
Moderate difficulty	Attempts to communicate basic needs
Severe difficulty	Feels no need to communicate with others

Imagination and play

Mild difficulty	Has learnt some of the rules governing play Lacks spontaneity
Moderate difficulty	Can play alongside peers and copy actions Play may be very repetitive
Severe difficulty	Lack of imagination Can't anticipate the future

**Please see the following pages to read about
additional features of autistic spectrum disorders.**

Additional features – strengths and weaknesses

There are other features that some people with autism will exhibit. These unusual aspects of thought and behaviour could cause major problems for the child in a mainstream classroom. However, some of these can also be strengths and understanding these will help the teacher to offer a suitable approach to teaching children with autism.

● **Restricted/obsessive interests** that can become 'all consuming', e.g. the child may become so obsessed with Thomas the Tank Engine that they may have difficulty focusing on anything else. It is always best to incorporate their interests into work if possible. Trying to get rid of an obsession is not usually recommended as another will probably replace it and this could be even worse! The child may be highly knowledgeable in their interest and will spend a long time finding out about the subject.

● **Obsessive desire for sameness** An overwhelming need to organise according to his or her own criteria, e.g. the child will enter the room and arrange all the items on your desk so that it is tidy! The child with autism prefers familiarity: a young child will probably go towards a new toy, but the child with autism will probably go away from the new to a familiar one. Children with autistic spectrum disorders do not like change as this creates uncertainty and leads to great anxiety.

● **Preoccupation/processing parts of objects rather than the whole** This is sometimes referred to as Central Coherence Deficit, e.g. the child will play with the wheels on a toy car rather than the car itself. The child will have difficulty connecting concepts and will need help to see the whole picture or overview.

● **Sensory distortion and hypersensitivity** The child may be very sensitive to stimuli which we do not even notice, e.g. the sound of a heater clicking on. They may also find noise distressing but talk in a very loud voice themselves.

● **Irrational fears/phobias** The child may be very frightened of objects or situations which to us do not appear threatening, e.g. may scream when the fan in the toilet makes a noise.

● **Repetitive body movements** such as flapping hands or rocking back and forth.

● **Repetitive speech** The child may repeat phrases or continue to talk about his or her particular interest, for example, unaware that others are not interested or that the subject is closed.

● **Repetitive routines** such as stacking blocks or lining up pencils over and over and over again. A liking or need for routine and order means that children with autism are often precise and accurate. The child will often produce very neat, careful work. He or she will often enjoy educational activities that are repetitive and which many children without autism would find boring.

● **Problems with joint attention** The child may not, for example, follow your gaze when you are pointing at an object. You may have problems with sharing and engaging attention and, once you have gained the child's attention, it is usually difficult to disengage.

● **Comprehension** Children with an autistic spectrum disorder are generally good at word recognition but often cannot understand what they read, e.g. the child will need help to find the relevant parts of the text in order to make sense of it.

● **Processing information** The child with an autistic spectrum disorder needs a lot longer to process language and it is important that teachers wait and allow the child time to answer a question.

● **Organisational skills** Children with an autistic spectrum disorder find it hard to create or initiate organisation but can follow an existing organisation, e.g. once routines and, work schedules are set up, the child with autism can easily follow them and they can give the child confidence and reduce stress.

● **Over stimulation** This can be a major cause of behaviour problems. Children with autism or Asperger syndrome can be hypersensitive to textures and will refuse to wear certain items of clothing as it is painful to them. If children are upset we are apt to increase stimulation by approaching them, talking to them, giving them comfort by touching them. For the child with autism this can increase anxiety. For a variety of reasons, anxiety can build up and up during the day and then the child 'blows'. It is therefore very important to find out what has been the trigger causing the unacceptable behaviour and try to avoid it.

● **Black and white view** Children with an autistic spectrum disorder may have problems empathising, e.g. they often do not realise other people have ideas or thoughts which differ from their own. This can lead to a misunderstanding, as the child does not see the need to explain a situation to the teacher or support assistant as he or she thinks they already know what has happened.

● **Islets of ability** Often uneven and erratic cognitive profiles are present, e.g. the child may excel at Science and be very poor in English. It is essential to do a variety of thorough assessments. If you are assessing and the child knows fact 'c' you can't assume the child knows 'a' and 'b'. Children with autism have difficulty concentrating and if the input to a lesson is auditory they will probably miss huge chunks of information.

● **Visual skills** Some people on the autistic spectrum say they think in pictures and many have good visual memories. Using a visual approach in the classroom is vital to enable the child to access the most from a lesson.

● **Sometimes have an excellent rote memory** Rote learning can be a useful approach for teachers to use. Staff need to be aware, however, that the child's expertise at reciting information can mask their lack of understanding about the topic.

Asperger syndrome/high functioning autism

Asperger syndrome is often associated with more able children on the autistic spectrum. These children are likely to have greater verbal skills and want to socialise more than children with classic Kanner's autism. It is generally agreed that children with a diagnosis of autism or Asperger syndrome both manifest the same triad of impairments that Lorna Wing described and therefore similar intervention techniques are helpful.

Pupils who fall into this category are likely to be able to achieve well academically, especially in more formal, less creative subjects, e.g. maths. They may, however, still need significant support in social situations, to maintain positive behaviour and with developing organisational skills. There are particular areas that may cause these children to have difficulty 'fitting in'. Problems making and sustaining friendships can be a great source of unhappiness and may lead to depression or an increase in aggressive behaviour.

Rigid thinking The children may find it hard to cope with changes and so strategies to help with transition times will need careful planning. They may have problems coping with the different behavioural expectations of the many staff they encounter during the day. Pupils with Asperger syndrome often have no understanding of tact and may just say what they are thinking! The pupil can often appear rude and staff will need to be made aware of this feature so that they can understand and make allowances.

Lack of social awareness Most children with Asperger syndrome want friends and would like to join in activities with their peers but they have poor social skills and often do not understand the peer group's rules or understand their behaviour. This means they can easily become a target for bullying and the school will need to be aware of the children who are particularly at risk. Some pupils may find eye contact difficult and this could result in them being thought of as rude. They are often not aware of people's personal space and may stand too close, which can make others feel uncomfortable or threatened. The pupil may not pick up meaning from others' body language and might not realise that someone is getting angry. Some children may have interests which can become obsessions and be unable to understand that others are not interested in the same thing.

Impaired communication skills Children with Asperger syndrome can often have a well developed vocabulary but still have difficulty communicating with others. They often take what is said to them literally and therefore may not understand jokes, sarcasm or metaphorical language. They frequently talk about their own interests and do not take account of the audience. Some children with Asperger syndrome talk in a loud voice with little intonation.

Poor co-ordination This can affect some children and they may also exhibit odd mannerisms. It can affect their performance in sport and could result in a child being bullied.

Adapting the curriculum and the learning environment

Why adapt the curriculum?

- Although children with autistic spectrum disorders are expected to follow the National Curriculum, consideration needs to be given to the way in which it is presented to children with autistic spectrum disorders.

- Consideration also needs to be given to the language and communication difficulties often associated with autistic spectrum disorders.

- Children with autistic spectrum disorders often do not pick up on implicit learning; they usually require key ideas and concepts to be explicitly taught.

- A lack of generalisation makes it difficult for children with autistic spectrum disorders to link concepts together and ideas may be understood in isolation (e.g. no understanding of multiplication as repeated addition, difficulty transferring knowledge to real life situations).

- An uneven cognitive profile may mean that there are areas of extreme strengths and weaknesses.

- Difficulty with comprehension of spoken/written language and literal interpretations could result in children 'getting the wrong end of the stick'.

- The 'triad of impairments' usually results in

  - an overwhelming need for structure

  - the need for support with social situations and

  - difficulties with receptive (what is heard) and expressive (what is said) language.

- Always be aware that the child may not realise that he/she is becoming anxious – look out for the triggers and early warning signs.

Ideas for making the curriculum 'user friendly' for children with autistic spectrum disorders

● **Teach specific topic vocabulary** Never assume that children have understood words and concepts, e.g. sequencing vocabulary (before, after etc.) is necessary in order to understand history in context.

● **Use visual support for new words/concepts** Display a key symbol alongside text in order to allow for visual consolidation and appeal to the visual learning style that many people with autism have.

● **Ensure structured activities with a clear start/finish** Children will then have a clear idea of exactly what work is required, including the amount before they begin. Where possible avoid open ended tasks, e.g. replace activities such as 'See how many … you can find' with 'Find 10 …' If this is not applicable, then use a time constraint, such as a 5 or 10 minute timer to signal the end of the activity. This will be helpful for those children who find switching attention and finishing activities difficult. A timer can be used throughout the day to give warnings for the end of any lesson or transition times, e.g. five minutes before assembly.

● **Present work in small 'chunks' of learning** Rather than expect the child to complete only part of a worksheet, cut out the specific task. This will eliminate any confusion over instructions that may be misinterpreted as well as anxiety over a task that appears too lengthy/difficult.

● **Be as practical and concrete as possible** This is especially important when introducing new ideas or skills. It may be a good idea to show finished examples of tasks, model use of equipment, or include adult role play to demonstrate exactly what is required.

● **Anticipate the day** Ensure that the activities displayed on the visual timetable can actually take place, or explain any necessary changes. It is extremely beneficial to children with autism to have a clear idea of what will be happening during the school day. A symbol such as a question mark could be inserted into the timetable to prepare for uncertain times like the school photographer coming or a fire practice.

● **Use straightforward language** This is extremely important when giving explanations and instructions. Quite often in the classroom we mix up the order of words spoken with the order of events by using sentences like, 'Before you get your reading book, remember to put your name on your work when you have finished it.' This style of speaking, which is natural and acceptable to most children can be particularly confusing for children with autism. An alternative instruction might be 'When you have finished, put your name on your work, then get your reading book.'

● **Avoid social and academic overload** Remember that any social/group work puts additional demands on the autistic spectrum disorder child – avoid planning lessons that are challenging both academically and socially, if the focus of the lesson involves working with others, then the actual task should be well within the ability of the autistic child. Academically demanding tasks may be better done in a quiet space independently.

The learning environment

Children with autistic spectrum disorders often have difficulty channelling their attention and are easily distracted. The classroom environment can have a dramatic effect on the child's behaviour and ability to learn.

Children with an autistic spectrum disorder will benefit from

● the classroom space being divided into distinct areas with clear physical boundaries. If an area is always used for work this helps the child to know what is expected of them in that area

● the teacher considering the seating arrangement of the class so that the child with an autistic spectrum disorder does not become distracted by others or by equipment

● an organised and uncluttered environment

● an individual working area

● clearly displayed visual reminders of expected behaviour

● well labelled and organised equipment

● easily accessible equipment for the task set and items that may be distracting placed out of sight

● expectations displayed in the different work areas.

If you have not got the space in your classroom to create individual work stations or 'office' areas, it is essential that the child has a named desk as a base. Try to use any available furniture such as bookcases to eliminate distractions. These bases will help not only children with an autistic spectrum disorder, but also others who find it difficult to concentrate in a classroom situation.

If you are working in an overcrowded classroom, try to find a quiet area elsewhere in the school that could be used as a 'haven' for the child with an autistic spectrum disorder. He or she could be hypersensitive to noise and become distressed and unable to cope if the noise levels become too high.

Use of support staff

Support staff can be indispensable for supporting children with autistic spectrum disorders. We have included below tried and tested ways in which support staff can offer assistance to the child.

- **Structuring work** Presenting work in small, manageable chunks, for example, by cutting up the worksheet or by dividing the work into numbered trays, making story frameworks and providing vocabulary lists.

- **Introducing and reinforcing key points of the lesson** Introducing, for example, new vocabulary and concepts; checking the child has understood what the teacher has said and that the follow up activity is understood, too.

- **Timetables and work schedules** Preparing and explaining these to the child at the beginning of the day/session including any changes that may be necessary.

- **Resources** Finding visual materials to support the lesson presented by the teacher and ensuring that all necessary equipment is available.

- **Modelling behaviour** by setting positive examples of e.g. 'Good sitting', 'Hands up': this could also be done by verbal reminder or showing a visual symbol.

- **Role playing** new situations or modelling use of equipment.

- **Managing individual education plans (IEPs)** Ensuring that the IEP (and behaviour plan if in place) is available for support staff to refer to. IEPs tend to work best when all support staff involved have had a chance to contribute their ideas.

- **Reading through an existing Social Story™** with the child or writing a new one if necessary (see section on Social Stories™ p26).

- **Work area organisation** Ensuring that the child's individual workstation or area has the necessary equipment and that it is clearly labelled.

- **Encouraging social relationships** Helping the child to form a friendship with a suitable peer; helping the child communicate in paired work sessions/group work.

- **Observations** Rather than tell you that there is a problem a child with an autistic spectrum disorder may display difficult behaviour. This is often the way the child will indicate something is wrong, so recording observations is a good way to discover triggers that may cause negative behaviour. Support staff's input is often invaluable when gathering such information for IEPs.

- **Establishing a 'circle of friends'** Supportive peers, who can provide support and act as positive role models in social situations or during lessons, and support staff can be instrumental in setting up this group. Alternatively, one or two children could be used as an informal 'buddy' to watch out for the child around school.

- **Support at playtimes, lunchtimes and transition times** Children with autistic spectrum disorders find unstructured times difficult to cope with and support staff may be needed to facilitate play or help explain social rules or expectations.

- **Training** Ensuring all staff in the school are aware of the needs of the child with an autistic spectrum disorder and have received training: staff supporting children with autistic spectrum disorders benefit from training and can offer invaluable input in sessions for others within the school.

Using visuals

Why use a visual approach?

Visual timetables enable children to

- follow the structure of the day without relying on verbal instructions or social cues

- have a point of continual reference to reduce anxiety and give them confidence and security

- avoid confrontation with adults – if it is time for an unpopular activity adults should refer the child to the timetable: 'the timetable says that we are going to do….'

- remove constant questioning about events in the day

- be prepared for changes

- link expected behaviours with timetabled activities.

How to implement visual timetables

- It works best if the timetable can be displayed in a central position for the whole class to see, perhaps going along the top of the whiteboard or displayed above it. If this isn't possible the child could have an individual version at their workplace.

- The teacher needs to run through the timetable either for the whole day or at the beginning of each session depending on the maturity of the child/class.

- Initially it may be necessary for the timetable to be referred to throughout the day. This helps the child to understand the pattern of the day and teaches them to refer to the timetable independently.

- We have included in the book timetable symbols that may be reproduced. These can be enlarged to form a class timetable.

- The symbols should be arranged either from left to right or top to bottom.

- To save time it is easier to arrange the daily symbols and photocopy and laminate them for one day, and then, if there are any necessary changes, to place the alternative over the top or mark it with a dry wipe marker pen. We have enclosed an example of a visual timetable on page 12.

- We have also enclosed a blank timetable (see page 13) so if a child needs his or her own individual timetable the symbols can be blu-tacked to the base board.

- Although visual timetables involve some effort to set up they are invaluable as they give the children structure and much needed confidence.

Work schedules

Work schedules are specific instructions for a particular task or activity.

Work schedules enable the children to

- know what work they are supposed to do, how much work there is, the order in which it is to be done, and what happens when it is finished

- learn the most important routines – the first one to teach is 'work first, and then play'. Other routines such as left to right and top to bottom give the children a systematic approach to tasks

- build positive routines

- work independently

- have a sense of achievement

- understand a set of instructions.

How to implement work schedules

We have included examples of work schedules in the book.

- The work schedule should be handed to the child after the lesson introduction. This will ensure that the child understands exactly what is expected of them.

- When children have completed one activity they can either remove the picture or cover it.

- Children can use smiley faces to cover the completed activity. This gives positive reinforcement.

- For younger children all the resources needed for the activity can be placed in trays and they are then immediately available and do not get lost.

- With younger children a lot of their work will be of a practical nature rather than paper and pencil tasks so it is very helpful to use trays or boxes to store it. By using trays every day the children learn the routine that they have to complete whatever is in them but it gives the teacher the flexibility to vary the activities and the length of time it will take to

complete. Consideration needs to be given to the length of time it will take to complete the tasks. Once children with autistic spectrum disorders have focused and started an activity they like to finish it and can get distressed if asked to stop before completion.

- For older children see through zip wallets containing activities could be used. This would again allow for the flexibility to vary the activities from day to day but the child has learnt the routine that they have to complete all the tasks in the folders.

> The symbols included in this book have been reproduced with kind permission from WIDGIT. It is possible to purchase a printed set of symbols or a word processing programme with symbols from Widgit Software Ltd, tel. 01223 425 558 email: info@widgit.com

An example of a visual timetable

morning

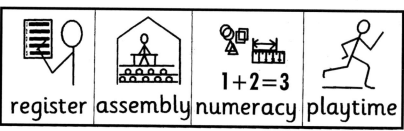

register | assembly | numeracy | playtime

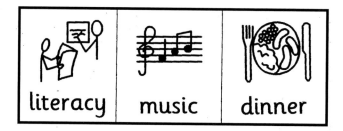

literacy | music | dinner

afternoon

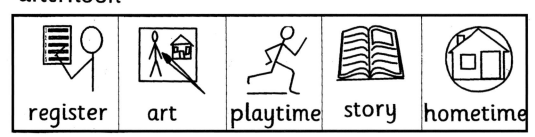

register | art | playtime | story | hometime

Symbols materials produced with Writing with Symbols 2000 and reproduced with permission from Widgit Software Ltd Tel 01223 425 558

Class Timetable

morning

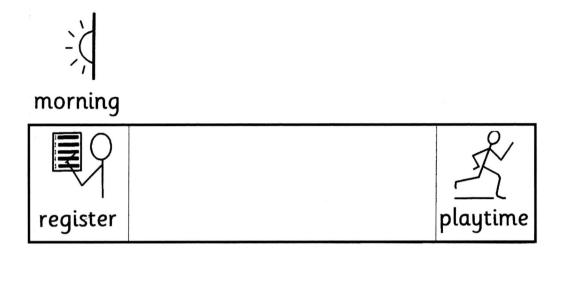

register

playtime

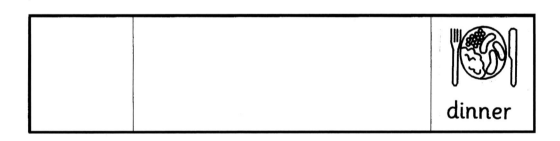

dinner

 afternoon

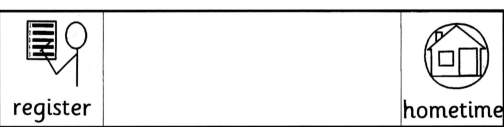

register

hometime

Cut out the appropriate visual symbols and bluetack on to the base board to make an individual timetable.

Symbols materials produced with Writing with Symbols 2000 and reproduced with permission from Widgit Software Ltd Tel 01223 425 558

Using visuals

Inclusion in the primary classroom: for children with autistic spectrum disorders   **13**

Picture Symbols

Visual timetable	morning	literacy	geography
Monday	afternoon	science	music
Tuesday	register	computer	P.E
Wednesday	assembly	D.T	group time
Thursday	play	art	apparatus
Friday	numeracy	history	circle time

Symbols materials produced with Writing with Symbols 2000 and reproduced with permission from Widgit Software Ltd Tel 01223 425 558

Inclusion in the primary classroom: for children with autistic spectrum disorders

Picture Symbols

writing	puzzles	choose	independent work
story	sand play	cooking	good listening
reading	water play	television	good sitting
playtime	visitor	home time	dinner time
singing	visitor	R.E	drawing
percussion	painting	games	cutting and sticking

*Symbols materials produced with Writing with Symbols 2000 and reproduced
with permission from Widgit Software Ltd Tel 01223 425 558*

Example of a work schedule suitable for a young child

activity   1

activity   2

show   work   to   adult

work   with   adult

choose

Symbols materials produced with Writing with Symbols 2000 and reproduced with permission from Widgit Software Ltd Tel 01223 425 558

Example of a work schedule suitable for Key Stage 2

<u>Independent</u>   <u>Literacy</u>   <u>Work</u>

1

Spellings

2

Dictionary work

3

Work sheet

4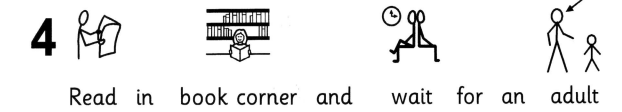

Read in book corner and   wait for an adult

Symbols materials produced with Writing with Symbols 2000 and reproduced with permission from Widgit Software Ltd Tel 01223 425 558

Promoting positive behaviour

In the classroom

Surroundings are very important to children with autism and can greatly influence behaviour in the classroom. The following considerations have proved to have a beneficial effect on the way in which children with an autistic spectrum disorder behave.

- Try to create areas in the classroom that are as 'distraction free' as possible so that children do not focus on or become absorbed by resources or activities that aren't connected with their task. This space should be used for independent work or for 'cooling off' or 'down time' when the child may become anxious or distressed, for example in a quiet corner of a room or facing a wall away from other children. Also, consider the amount and type of children or adults who will need to pass by and wherever possible eliminate this 'traffic'

- Mark clearly with a visual symbol if necessary where you want the child to be in the school or classroom. This will lessen the need to explain seating arrangements and confrontations that may arise out of uncertainty about where to sit.

- You may need to pay close attention to group times or carpet times if these cause particular difficulties. Where appropriate sit the child with another adult or 'buddy'. Make sure the child is not within reach of any enticing equipment to fiddle with. Give the child a cushion to sit on or put a sticker on the carpet where you want the child to sit. If sitting still becomes a problem then try using a 'fidget' toy that you have provided.

- Read the section in this book on 'Using visuals'. Set and display behaviour targets. These may need to be in more than one area of the classroom. As with all targets, make sure they are realistic. Remember to display what reward the child will be working towards.

- Refer to the expected behaviour throughout the school. See the examples in this book (page 21 and page 22) of our 'Good sitting' posters, which could be used in assemblies.

- Children with autism often do not pick up on general classroom routines and need to have these clearly displayed. In effect they often learn routines rather than pick up on social cues.

- Always try to follow the visual timetable. If a confrontation occurs, try to avoid turning this into a personal argument by stating for example, 'The timetable (as opposed to 'I') says it's time for literacy.'

- Never underestimate the power of consistency! If all adults working with the child agree upon and use short, set phrases then this is likely to have much more of an impact and will be easier for the child to understand, as there is no longer a requirement to process different aspects of language. Even if a slightly different phrase is used the child will have to process the information again.

- Find out in advance what the child's special interests are and use these as motivators. Be aware that these may appear different or unusual, for example collecting paper clips or stacking unifix. If it works to motivate the child then use it (within reason!). It is important that any reward system is known to all the adults and used consistently.

● Structure each lesson and try to provide an overview of the whole topic in advance so that it is clear what the overall aim is. This could lessen any anxiety the child may have about what is happening next and will also be helpful to put future learning in context.

● For times of the day when listening and attention may be required, teach and use the 'Good listening' page included in this book (see page 20). Warn children in advance that they will have to listen and constantly refer to these rules and praise when they are followed. This strategy is always useful in every class as many children need to improve their listening skills. It is important to explain to the child what you mean by 'good listening'. It is not obvious to them to give eye contact or use body language to indicate that they are listening and for many children with autism this is a difficult skill.

● Use the child's name – this sounds obvious but often in a classroom we give out general instructions and wonder why not everybody follows them. Often children with autism will not realise the instruction applies to them and so some negative behaviour can be avoided if the teacher makes sure the child has heard and understood directions. Always welcome a child with an autistic spectrum disorder on arrival by name to encourage positive social interaction.

Unstructured times of the day

Children with autistic spectrum disorders can find unstructured times of the day difficult to cope with. They may need support at playtimes, lunchtimes and in lessons that involve change, e.g. PE.

● It would be a good idea if potential 'trouble spots' (e.g. lining up for lunch, getting ready for PE) are identified and then strategies in this book could be used or adapted to suit individual children.

● Try to gather as much information from observations as possible. This often reveals a pattern around certain activities or transition times where change or uncertainty has given rise to negative behaviour. Try noting down what the behaviour is (e.g. kicking) and then consider when the behaviour occurs and where it occurs. This should provide some likely triggers. If necessary, try using our behaviour plan to ensure a consistent approach and review it (this can be done quickly during a brief chat) as often as possible to ensure the approaches or triggers are still relevant. See example of behaviour support plan (p30) and blank (p31).

● An adult may have to suggest activities that they can engage in whilst at play, e.g. playing a playground game or using play equipment and modelling appropriate ways in which to approach others and join in a game. This could be reinforced with the use of a Social Story™.

● If a child with autism becomes stressed then increasing the amount of interaction/attention (as one normally does) can make matters worse. So often the well-intentioned adult can actually be contributing to major incidents unknowingly by not allowing the child any time or space to cool off. It may be advisable to set a timer so that the child is aware there is a limit to this cooling off period and when to expect adult attention again.

● Teaching children with autism to use a set phrase or display a visual (e.g. a special picture card) in order to get help or to let people know they are becoming angry may be necessary. The child can then seek help where appropriate and not continue to become more and more frustrated, which can often lead to temper tantrums that apparently 'come from nowhere' but in fact stem from a difficulty in gaining help at the right time.

We have included a bank of ideas which can be used as targets in the child's individual education plan (IEP), see pages 34-37 and two examples of charts to develop motivation on pages 23 and 25.

To do good listening you must

Do good sitting

Stay quiet

Look at the teacher talking

Think about what they say

Symbols materials produced with Writing with Symbols 2000 and reproduced with permission from Widgit Software Ltd Tel 01223 425 558

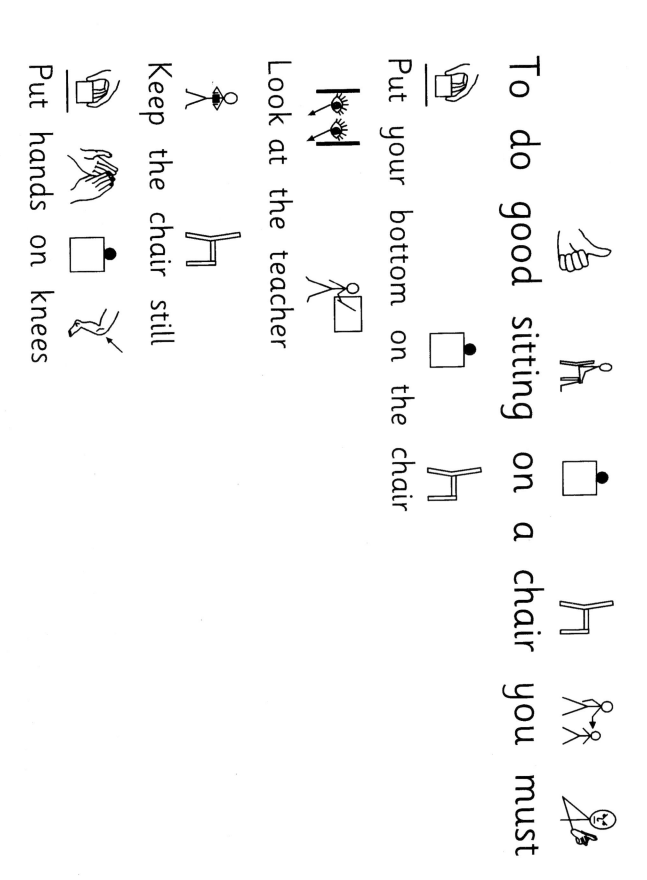

To do good sitting on a chair you must

Put your bottom on the chair

Look at the teacher

Keep the chair still

Put hands on knees

Symbols materials produced with Writing with Symbols 2000 and reproduced with permission from Widgit Software Ltd Tel 01223 425 558

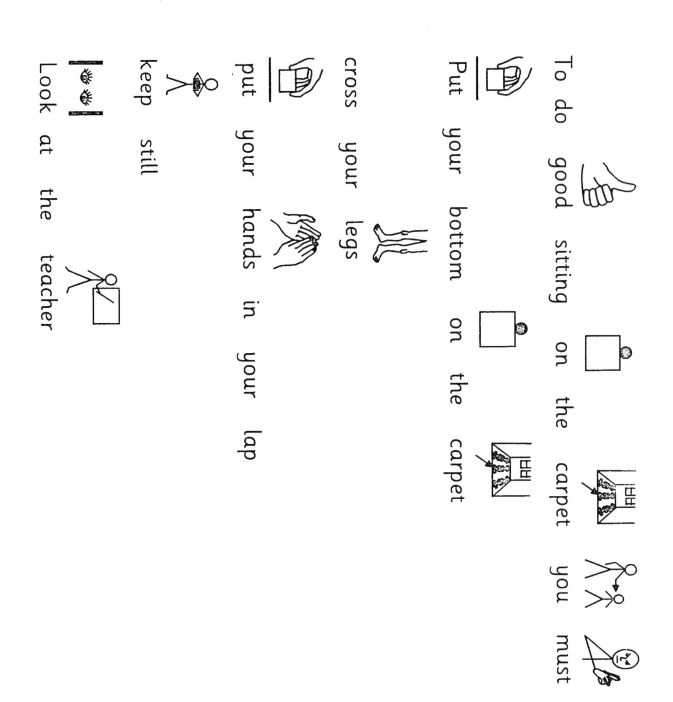

To do good sitting on the carpet you must

Put your bottom on the carpet

cross your legs

put your hands in your lap

keep still

Look at the teacher

Symbols materials produced with Writing with Symbols 2000 and reproduced with permission from Widgit Software Ltd Tel 01223 425 558

name ....

My   Star   Chart

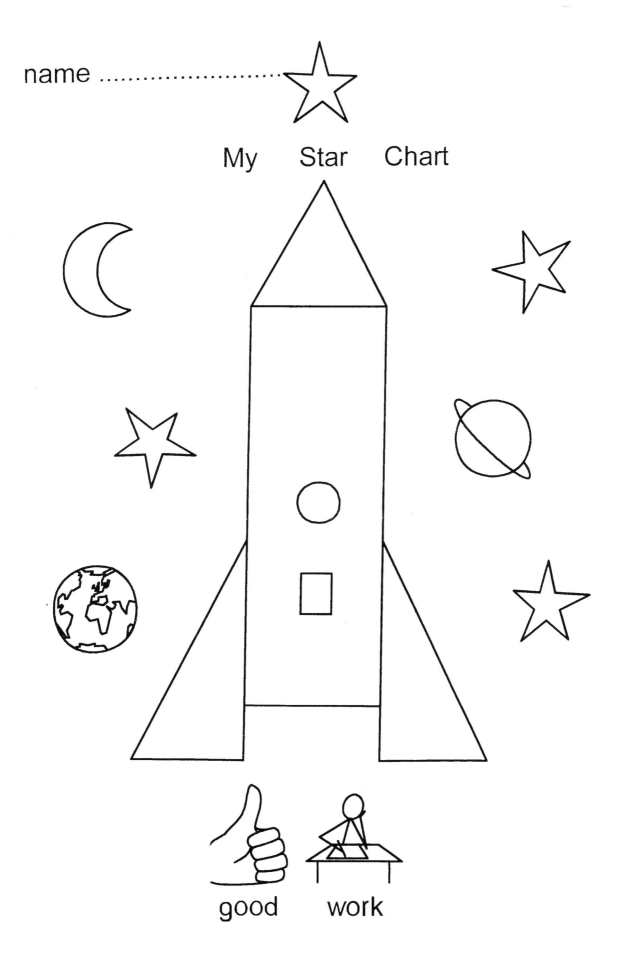

good   work

Symbols materials produced with Writing with Symbols 2000 and reproduced with permission from Widgit Software Ltd Tel 01223 425 558

_____'s Behaviour Chart

Behaviour	☺	😐	☹			☺	😐	☹			☺	😐	☹
Mon				B					L				
Tues				R					U				
Wed				E					N				
Thur				A					C				
Fri				K					H				

If I get _____ ☺ I can _____

Social Stories™

Social Stories™ were an idea developed by Carol Gray in America in 1991. One of Carol's earliest stories was written for a child in P.E. who did not understand the game so she wrote a special story. Social Stories™ are read to children frequently. The goal of each Social Story™ is to share social information. In many cases, this means describing what is occurring around the child and why. The result is often an improvement in the child's situation.

Why use Social Stories™?

Social Stories™ may

- describe social situations and desired behaviour without the usual teacher/pupil interaction

- teach routines and help the child understand, anticipate and/or handle changes effectively

- break down situations, concepts or skills into understandable steps or units, teaching one thing at a time

- help the child learn new, positive responses to situations that previously resulted in anxiety, social withdrawal or negative emotional responses

- be used to help children understand and cope with a forthcoming event

- help the child understand and respond more effectively to new situations.

We have included in this book an example of a Social Story™ that we have used to encourage sharing. This story is printed on two pages but with young children we have found it very helpful to write each sentence on a separate page and make the story into a book.

For more examples of Social Stories™ Carol Gray has written a very helpful book entitled *My Social Stories Book*, published by Jessica Kingsley ISBN 1 85302 950 5.

The following guidelines are reproduced with kind permission from Carol Gray and taken from her website: www.thegraycenter.org. There is also a range of other useful information on this site and it is well worth a visit.

Please note that Carol Gray refers to autistic spectrum disorders using the common abbreviation ASD.

Writing your own Social Story™

Step 1. Picture the goal The general goal of Social Stories™ is to *share accurate social information, to describe more than direct.* Picturing the goal requires a parent/professional to translate social information into meaningful text and illustrations. In many cases, this means describing abstract concepts and ideas with visual, concrete references and images. Therefore, while the end result of a Social Story™ may be a change in the response of the person with an autistic spectrum disorder, the *first priority – the goal – is always to share relevant social information in a meaningful way.*

Step 2. Gather information Once a clear picture of the goal is established, the parent/professional gathers information about the topic. This includes *where* the situation occurs, *who* is involved, *how* long it lasts, *how* it begins and ends, *what* occurs, and *why.* In addition, information about the learning style, reading ability, attention span, and interests of the person with ASD is collected. This information is gathered by direct observation and interviewing those involved with the person with ASD: parents, professionals, and if possible, the person with ASD.

Step 3. Tailor the text The author customizes the text to the learning style, needs, interests, and abilities of the person with ASD. This results in a *Social Story™*, a story with the following defining characteristics:

- An introduction, body, and conclusion.

- Answers to "wh" questions, including *who* is involved, *where* a situation occurs, *what* is happening, *how* it happens, and *why.*

● Written from a first person perspective, i.e. as though the person with ASD is describing the event or concept, and occasionally from a third person perspective, like a newspaper article.

● Positive language and positively stated responses and behaviors; if a reference to a negative behavior is made, it is done with extreme caution and in a more general third person – rather than specific first or second person – manner. For example, *Sometimes people may unintentionally say something to hurt another person's feelings. This is a mistake.*

● Up to four basic types of Social Story™ sentences: *descriptive, perspective, affirmative,* and *directive;* that occur in a proportion specified by The Basic Social Story Ratio (0–1 directive sentences for every 2–5 descriptive, perspective, and/or affirmative sentences). Possibly up to six sentence types, including in addition control and/or cooperative sentences, that occur in a proportion specified by the Complete Social Story Ratio (0–1 directive and/or control sentences for every 2–5 descriptive, perspective, affirmative, and/or cooperative sentences).

● Literal accuracy (can be interpreted literally without altering intended meaning of text and illustrations), with use of "insurance policy" words like *usually* and *sometimes* to ensure that accuracy.

● Use of alternative vocabulary when needed. (For example, the first word in each of the following pairs may elicit anxiety, so it is followed by possible alternative word or words: different = *another,* change = *replace,* new = *better or another.*)

● Use of text consistent with the personal learning characteristics of the person with ASD. For young children, concrete, easy to understand text enhanced by visual supports is often used (translating abstract concepts into tangible, visually based terminology and illustration). For older or more advanced people with ASD, a Social Story™ may take a format similar to a newspaper article, with advanced text and corresponding tables or graphs that enhance the meaning of the text.

● Illustrations (if needed) that reflect consideration of the age and personal learning characteristics of the person with ASD.

● A style and format that is motivating, or reflects the interests of, the person with ASD.

Step 4: Teach with the title The title of a Social Story™ states the overall meaning or "gist" of the Social Story™, following the applicable characteristics listed in Step 3. References to any behaviours – positive or negative – are rarely a part of a Social Story™ title. Sometimes, a title may be stated as a question, with the story answering the question. Whether as a statement or question, the title identifies and reinforces the most important information in the Social Story™.'

Helpful Hints

● Present each Social Story™ in a calm, comfortable tone. Never present a Social Story™ to a child who is already upset. Never use a Social Story™ as a punitive consequence, or as a consequence in any way of negative behaviour.

● After sharing the Social Story™ with the child, let the child show it to others. Sharing the Social Story™ helps the child to learn that everyone has the same expectations.

● Other adults will also be able to refer to the Social Story™ and help the child when he/she has a problem.

● If possible, read the Social Story™ prior to a situation the child has difficulty coping with.

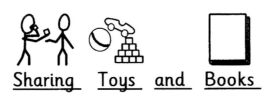

Sharing Toys and Books

Sometimes children play with toys or read books.

Many children like to share the toys and books.

They may take turns or play together.

Sharing toys and books is a friendly thing to do.

Symbols materials produced with Writing with Symbols 2000 and reproduced with permission from Widgit Software Ltd Tel 01223 425 558

Promoting positive behaviour

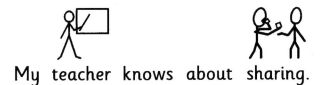

My teacher knows about sharing.

She will help me to learn to share.

I will try to share the toys and books.

Sharing is a good thing to do.

Example of completed behaviour support plan

Description of Behaviour/ Triggers	Preventative Strategies	Early Interaction	Adult Intervention
**** finds it difficult to sit next to another child and play with the same equipment. When another child approaches **** to join in his game **** becomes agitated and either walks away or takes the toy from the other child.	Practise sharing in situations that have been set up by adult. Adult to supervise and play with the pair. In circle time introduce rules for playing with a friend.	Show visual symbol indicating 'good sharing' Adult to model how to ask for a toy.	Adult to join group and organise turn taking and help negotiation.
When it is time to change activity **** gets excited and becomes noisy, frequently banging equipment.	Introduce a Social Story™ to remind him to be quiet. Read Social Story™ before activity to reinforce appropriate behaviour.	When **** becomes noisy adult to remain silent but hold up 'quiet' symbol. Adult to give **** a verbal warning.	Adult to remove toy/activity until **** is quiet. **** to go out of the room with an adult until quiet.
**** wants to be 'first'. He wants to be the first to participate in a chosen activity and he also wants to be the class leader every time.	Refer to pictorial timetable or work schedule at the beginning of a session remove or cover pictures of activities when completed. Tell him clearly if he is not first today.	1. Adult to use phrase '........ later' 2. Adult to ask **** 'when do you do..... today?'	Adult to bar ****'s way if he tries to push to the front and remind him to be quiet and wait his turn.

Behaviour support plan

Description of Behaviour/Triggers	Preventative Strategies	Early Interaction	Adult Intervention

Example of completed overview – Pupil Profile

Name: ***** **Class:** **** **Year:** ** **Date:** **/**/**

STRENGTHS –

- Friendly towards adults
- Very motivated if task/topic interests him
- Can work in small groups
- Enjoys computer work
- Good range of interests
- Good range of vocabulary
- Able child who can achieve with encouragement
- Motivated by rewards/sanctions
- Can display good social skills

WEAKNESSES –

- Easily distracted
- Can be difficult to motivate
- Easily bored
- Can decide reward is 'not worth it'
- Dismissive/negative

OPPORTUNITIES FOR DEVELOPMENT –

- Group work
- Independent (of adult) tasks
- Creative writing
- Problem solving
- Reading fluency/expression
- Personal projects
- Social skills
- Anger management

BARRIERS TO LEARNING –

- Becomes easily frustrated if task is perceived too difficult
- Requires significant adult support if task is perceived difficult
- Becomes angry if situation is perceived as unfair
- Can be very disruptive
- Occasionally aggressive towards adults/children

Overview – Pupil Profile

Name:	Class:	Year:	Date:

STRENGTHS –	WEAKNESSES –
OPPORTUNITIES FOR DEVELOPMENT –	BARRIERS TO LEARNING –

IEP TARGET BANK

Concern	Target
Group Time	• To follow 'Good Listening' poster • To follow 'Good Sitting' poster • To use 'hands up' and not interrupt • To answer _____ questions appropriately when asked directly by an adult • To answer visually supported questions in full sentences • To participate in group activities/register time for _____ minutes • To sit quietly and not make inappropriate noises • To take turns when speaking e.g. in circle time • To ask a question or make a comment at an appropriate time • • • • •

Concern	Target
Independent Work	• To work independently for _____ minutes
	• To collect the correct resources and equipment
	• To complete one activity independently
	• To begin independent work when asked to do so
	• To finish working independently when asked to do so
	• To respond to a timed warning for change of activity
	• To follow a work schedule
	• To follow routine for transition times
	•
	•
	•
	•
	•
	•
	•

Concern	Target
Working with others	• To begin a conversation by asking an appropriate question
	• To comprehend and accept a whole class system for turn taking or sharing
	• To follow structured and visually supported activities for turn taking
	• To follow individual/class timetable
	• To follow adult direction and to develop co-operative skills e.g. _____
	• To attract a person's attention by saying their name before continuing to talk to them
	• To establish eye contact with whoever is talking
	• To maintain a short conversation on a topic chosen by someone else
	• To ask specific questions for clarification
	• To comment appropriately on an activity
	• To answer specific questions directly
	• To close/finish a conversation when appropriate
	• To finish activities when asked to do so
	• To respond consistently to a timed warning for the end of activities
	• To wait for adult attention
	• To attract adult attention appropriately
	• To accept when a rule is broken and sanction applied
	• To listen to warnings
	• To ask for help/clarification by using a set phrase or signal
	• To understand figurative speech/idioms
	• To request an item/activity politely
	• To follow a positive model for interaction with at least one other child
	• To complete one structured activity within a small group

Concern	Target
Play/lunch times	• To tell adults about other children's unacceptable behaviour and not to retaliate • To avoid touching other children inappropriately in the playground • To share playground equipment with one other child • To ask an adult for help • To remember to look after personal effects e.g. coat • To ask before leaving canteen/playground e.g. to go to the toilet • To stay in the right area in the playground • To follow a given Social Story™ • To sustain a play activity for _____ minutes • To suggest/initiate a play activity with another child • To follow established routines

Sources of information

National Autistic Society Head Office
393 City Road,
London
EC1V 1NG
Tel: 020 7833 2299
Email: nas@nas.org.uk
Autism Helpline: 0845 070 4004
Training and Consultancy: 0115 911 3363
Conferences and Events: 0115 911 3367
Publications: 020 7903 3595
Website: www.autism.org.uk

The National Autistic Society (NAS) produces a comprehensive publications catalogue: telephone the NAS publications department to obtain a copy, or check the publications section of the NAS website. The National Autistic Society publishes useful books and leaflets on autism and Asperger syndrome and it also provides the Autism Helpline for parents, carers and people with autism and Asperger syndrome.

The NAS Information Centre is a resource for professional and research enquiries, and the website provides a wealth of information, including fact sheets, for researchers. Visit www.autism.org.uk/infocentre

Training courses and conferences on issues of interest are organised throughout the UK (see telephone number above).

Useful publications and resources

Approaches to autism*
Published by The National Autistic Society 2007
ISBN 978 1905 722 211
This guide outlines different approaches to autism and gives details of where to find out further information.

* Available from NAS Publications,
Tel 020 7903 3595

Asperger syndrome – practical strategies for the classroom: a teachers's guide*
By Leicester City Council and Leicestershire County Council
Published by The National Autistic Society 1998
ISBN 978 1 899280 018
A very practical and easy to use guide for teachers and support staff, looking at the difficulties which children with Asperger syndrome may experience and effective strategies to help.

The Complete guide to Asperger's syndrome*
By Tony Attwood
Published by Jessica Kingsley Publishers 2007
ISBN 978 1 843106 692
Tony Attwood's considerable experience of more than 25 years as a specialist in the field of Asperger syndrome makes this a truly authoritative book on the subject.

The autistic spectrum: a guide for parents and professionals*
By Lorna Wing
Published by Constable and Robinson 1996
ISBN 978 1 84119 674 9
This key work is widely acknowledged as the definitive book on the subject.

Autism: how to help your young child*
Published by The National Autistic Society 1998
ISBN 978 1 899280 65 0
Leicester City Council and the Fosse Health Trust
Primarily aimed at parents, this book also contains useful information which can help with the triad of impairments and behaviour.

Can I tell you about Asperger syndrome? A guide for family and friends*
Jude Welton
Published by Jessica Kingsley Publishers, 2003
ISBN 978 1 84310 206 9
Adam is a ten year old boy with Asperger syndrome. He explains his talents and difficulties as if talking to school friends and family. Jane Telford's cheerful pictures bring Adam's words to life.

Challenging behaviour and autism: making sense – making progress*

Philip Whitaker
Published by The National Autistic Society, 2001
ISBN 978 1 899280 5 13
Offers jargon-free advice and practical strategies for preventing or managing the sorts of challenging behaviour most likely to be encountered. With detailed case studies and key tips that allow it to be used as a quick reference.

Classroom and playground*

Perepa Prithvi
Published by The National Autistic Society, 2005
ISBN   978 1 899280 5 75
A booklet aimed at school staff with little experience of working with younger children with ASD. The strategies are covered in detail and also in point form for ease of reference.

Developing pupils' social communication skills*

Penny Barratt, Julie Border, Helen Joy, Alison Parkinson, Mo Potter and George Thomas
Published by David Fulton 2001
This book offers a wide variety of simple but effective strategies for developing communication and social skills.

Don't take it so literally!

Danielle M. Ledger
Published by ECL Publications 1991
ECL Publications, PO Box 26, Youngtown, Arizona 85363, USA
Tel 00 1 623 974 4560
www.eclpublications.com
A variety of idioms presented in a cartoon 'fun manner' that can be photocopied and used to teach whatever specific idioms are needed. Fun to use and a good discussion point for group work – dispels any myths children may have created around hearing and misunderstanding idioms – essential for young children or those at primary schools who have language disorders.

Everybody is different*

By Fiona Bleach
Published by The National Autistic Society 2001
ISBN 1 899280 37 5
An illustrated book for school friends or brothers or sisters. It explains the characteristics of autism and suggests ways to support.

How Joshua learned – making sense of the world with autism*

Joshua Love, aged 8
Published by The National Autistic Society, 2007
ISBN   978 1 905722 3 41
A self-help book, aimed at children aged 3-7 with ASD, their parents and teachers. Joshua explains visual supports and other strategies that have helped him.

Meeting the needs of children with autistic spectrum disorders*

By Rita Jordan and Glenys Jones
Published by David Fulton
ISBN   1 853465 82 8
The authors suggest reasons for the way children with autism behave and give guidance on ways to respond.

My brother is different*

By Louise Gorrod. Full colour illustrations by Becky Carver.
Published by The National Autistic Society 1997
ISBN 1 899280 50 2
This picture book, suitable for the 3-7 age range, explains the behaviour of a child with autism in very simple terms.

My social stories book*

By Carol Gray
Published by Jessica Kingsley 2002
ISBN 1 85302 950 5
Social stories are very effective in teaching social skills. The book provides many examples of social stories and is very useful if you want to try writing your own.

Positive people

Claire Moore and Tina Rae
Lucky Duck Publishing
ISBN 1 873942 92 3
Tel 0117 973 2881
A structured programme with photocopiable worksheets and activities aimed at developing social skills and raising 'other awareness' and breaking the cycle of negative self-esteem, attention seeking and poor behaviour. This is suitable for able year two children upwards and throughout key stage two. Good for starting a social skills group or for circle time.

* Available from NAS Publications,
Tel 020 7903 3595

Semantic-pragmatic language disorder

Charlotte Firth and Katherine Venkatesh
Speechmark ISBN 0 86388 329 X
Tel 0121 666 7878
Although not strictly for children with autism, many of the explanations and activities will be useful, especially with younger children. Also a good resource bank of activities that can be given to parents who want to support their child's development with specific activities at home.

The social use of language programme

Wendy Rinaldi
Published by Learn Communicate Publications
18 Dorking Road, Chilworth, Surrey GU4 8NR
Tel 01483 268 825
This is a series of stories that deals with basic social skills and matters arising from communication difficulties, for example listening and taking messages. The books are designed to be user friendly and are particularly beneficial for children in the primary school.

Socially speaking

Alison Schroeder
Published by LDA 2001
LDA, Duke Street, Wisbech PE13 2AE
Tel 01945 463 441
An invaluable guide to teaching social skills from the very basic e.g. eye contact to the more sophisticated e.g. ordering meals in a restaurant! Can be used as a whole programme or for specific areas- includes photocopiable resources – essential!

Special educational needs: a guide for parents and carers of children with autistic spectrum disorders *

Carolyn Waterhouse and the NAS Advocacy for Education team
Published by The National Autistic Society, 2006
ISBN 978 1 905722 0 37. This very helpful guide explains the law relating to special educational needs, additional supports, who provides them and how to access them. It includes useful timescales and pointers.

Teaching children with autism to mind-read: a practical guide*

By Patricia Howlin, Simon Baron-Cohen and Julie Hadwin
Published by John Wiley and Sons Ltd 1998
ISBN 978 0 471976 23 3
This book describes the authors' own intervention programme and offers practical guidelines for helping children with autism to understand emotions.

* Available from NAS Publications,
Tel 020 7903 3595

Teaching young children with autistic spectrum disorders to learn*

By Liz Hannah. Illustrations by Steve Lockett.
Published by the National Autistic Society
ISBN 978 1 899280 32 2
This is a practical guide for parents and staff in mainstream schools and nurseries. It contains lots of useful ideas to support and teach children with an autistic spectrum disorder.

Thinking in pictures*

By Temple Grandin
Published by Vintage Books 1996
ISBN 978 0 679 77289 7
This is a personal account of what it is like to think, feel and experience the world if you have autism.

Think it! Say it!

Luanne Martin
Communication Skill Builders
ISBN 0 88450 570 7
A series of line drawings depicting everyday situations with ideas and suggestions to work on specific areas of language and communication skills. Can be used at many different levels from very basic commenting to refining, reasoning and organisational skills. An excellent resource for small group work with children who need support with any area of communication and social understanding.

Tobin learns to make friends*

By Diane Murrell
Published by Future Horizons Inc. 2001
ISBN 978 1 885 477 79 8
Illustrated in colour, this book helps young children with Asperger syndrome and high-functioning autism to learn the rules of friendship.

What is Asperger syndrome and how will it affect me?*

NAS Autism Helpline
Published by The National Autistic Society 1999
ISBN 978 1 899280 14 8
Aimed at 8-13 year olds, this booklet explains Asperger syndrome in jargon free terms to young people with the condition.

When my worries get too big: a relaxation book for children with autism spectrum disorders*

Kari Dunn Buron
UK version published by The National Autistic Society
ISBN 978 1 90572 2 50 1
Aimed at 5-8 year olds, children who use the simple strategies presented in this delightful book will find themselves relaxed and ready to work or play.

Computer program

Writing with symbols

Widgit Software Ltd

Tel 01223 425 558

www.widgit.com

The symbols used in this pack were reproduced with kind permission from Widgit software. The computer program is invaluable for making visual timetables and work schedules. It can also be used to support writing and for making worksheets.

Video

Ask me about Asperger syndrome*

Published by Jessica Kingsley Publishers 2000

ISBN 1 85302 987 4

Teachers, psychologists, speech therapists and parents describe the impairments that affect pupils with Asperger syndrome and offer practical suggestions and strategies for working with them.

Understanding Asperger syndrome*

Produced by the Royal Children's Hospital, Victoria, 2000

This video which is accompanied by an extensive set of notes, contains information on diagnosis and assessment, typical behaviour characteristics of children with Asperger syndrome (including case studies), management and teaching strategies.

Websites

www.autism.org.uk The National Autistic Society website

www.mugsy.org/wendy This website is designed by Wendy Lawson. Wendy has an autistic spectrum disorder. She is a poet and a writer, sharing her understanding of autism with others.

* Available from NAS Publications,
Tel 020 7903 3595

Notes